EROS TO GODHEAD

EROS TO GODHEAD

Sutras of Healing and Ecstasy from the Infant

Thom Namayá

Celo Valley Books
Burnsville, North Carolina

This book was produced by
Celo Book Production Service
346 Seven Mile Ridge Road
Burnsville NC 28714

Eros to Godhead may be ordered by sending $6.00 for each copy you wish to order to: Mr. Thom Namayá, Box 153, Upper Nyack, New York 10960.

Poster size copies of individual poems within this book are also available.

Library of Congress Catalog Card Number 90-84955
ISBN 0-923687-08-4

CONTENTS

EROS TO GODHEAD

the journey!

... love, enchantment, celebration, and savoring the simple joyfulness of the god or goddess within each one of us:

it is about the splendor and pain of children, the dharma of eating peanut-butter, and the bliss of being alive:

it speaks of the ridiculous, the sublime, and the sensuous:

it is seeing the short-comings, the injustice, isolation, the relationships that never quite worked, and knowing this is also part of the journey.

i drive along a heavily wooded country road in the early autumn as the sun-light pours through my window,
    and feel the intense erotic-godhead bliss;

i celebrate that spirit!

Eros to Godhead, the journey each one of us creates.

come, let us dance and play !

Let us discover and celebrate this life.

GAIA

1.

What was the sound of a seed
    first
bursting to light?

And the ash swallow
    when she ascended
into being?

What was the sound of her flight?

What was the elegance
    of lightning
before it turned to fire?

And how did
    the ocean birth
a tide — before
    the weight of human sorrow?

In still memory

I hear the incandescent thrill
    of Spring's first green

and the wind's sensuous roar
    across lonely shores.

2.

In the cold slash of
    winter

I remember the first snow

and the sensation, near delicious,
    on the frozen virgin earth.

I hear Gaia breathe
        inside these shriveled cells

and ache to feel sunlight.

This human loneliness needs to
remember

how Gaia spoke when she first breathed
        and whispered to life
                this soul...

frail and precious
        as a swallow's

infant voice.

thirst

alone. accepted that. who this person is — alone.

not isolated — just alone.
women, I watch, hunger, and then pray.
            somewhere between eros and godhead,
this mendicant wanders.
winter deepens, a voice enters through the phone... I breathe
        and hold to nothing, and yet for the enormous joy of holding
            you close. I hunger!

we feast and I awaken miles above — sublimely asleep
    in acres of sheets.

I am frightened sometimes — when I 'm not alone. Am I losing
    myself? Am I whole or tumbling through some torn cloud?
A fool who tries to love? Does he even know how?

when will she say good-by?

we undress with eager fingers — searching. drinking! is there one
place i've yet to touch? one delicious secret still to be revealed?

in the middle of the afternoon. hungry. wanting to hold her. no
thoughts. no words. just here, in this hour.

hold me. i'm starting to fall.

COMMON FEAST

We meet with common hunger
In the need to nurture and create.

In this room with hearth and wide serenity
I lay these offerings on the table.

We eat and feast,

Upon voiceless sorrows —
ghosted memories
    and
this unclaimed joy —
    Liberated!

I dip my soul into the feast
    and savor
each minim of sorrow
    insight and knowing;
and private chamber of doubt

In each, lies a seed of Truth
    Waiting to be offered and devoured.
Revelation in each morsel tasted.
    Ecstasy with each veil shredded!

Souls lightened by the common feast
In this simple hunger to nurture and heal.

LOVE

today,
I put on
my socks.

tomorrow
I will change
them.

THANKS FOR THE LEAVES

I often wonder about god
 and how she made the world.

I imagine that one bright morning
        Gaia — Great Mother Spirit of the Universe
            woke up
stretched her arms wide —
        Y a w n e d —

had a cup of coffee and

contemplated what she would
  make that day.
I see the leaves of this elm tree and think,
        what a splendid thing it is —
leaves full broad-palmed and deep green....

Did Gaia Mother Spirit of the Universe plan it so?
Or did she, in some imagined bliss,
  imagine something...
                        sensuous
                            & delightful
    that moved with the wind?

Thus in a single revery
        created waves
that roll on to shores
        and leaves that sway gracefully free.

Then it occurs,
  if a leaf was
as free as it wanted to be
        it would be —
        perhaps — a bird?

Yes! And so it was
        and soared to heaven
to see the Mother face of Gaia,

beaming a delightful smile
        in all that she created.

MON NOM — LE PETIT PRINCE — QUI CHERCHE

I cannot walk through these city streets like you.
Cannot wander.
Will not empty this self out on to
    clean white china platters;
and damn straight refuse to march.

... while the arms move on
and heads turn to catch sight
of wind and sky,
and seasons unfold with
erotic awakening...

I cannot walk through these city streets like you.
Cannot wander.
Will not choose to empty this self out on to
    the narrow scrubbed corner
and the broad white
    linen sheets.

I am not made of wood or stone.
Nor formed by whim or incantation of
    evening tides,
but molded and unspun —
    woven and then abandoned
by the falling — rising breath of
    a woman who sleeps, dream-bound beside me.

I am this child and innocent man,
le petit prince qui cherche!
Warrior of the heart! Unvanquished by mortal
    abuse, common fears, or subtle variations
        on truth!

With a bold veracity
I will astound you and most importantly,
    myself.
By the certainty
    and sure step that leads on.

Not callowed by doubts and fears,
   that consume these tender expectations,
but made certain and clear eyed
   by a world of innocence
        yet
   untouched—

   unheld,

   and
too rarely loved.

CARPE DIEM!

When I kiss and lick
    the round laughing belly
of an infant,
    I hold miracle in my eyes.

We have dreamed a life,
    of such wondrous things.

Yet, I had been too long captivated by the
    spell and artful intentioned weaving
of the human will,

and failed to hold that which was
    indeed, precious—

Time.   Love.   And this, moment.

Life! Too long hidden in a shadow of pained isolation.
Until today,
    at last fed up with the lies,
     and in a shout of freedom from the root of my soul,
Ripped off my clothes and lay naked under the carefree
        erotic perfection,
    of sunlight, on a cool breezed afternoon.

We have dreamed a life of such wondrous things,
    and yet—have stood emptied for all our travail.

I have seen the cancer wards
    and held the dying in my arms.
I have rocked them to sleep and blessed them
    as they moved on.

And when it is my turn to leave
    I will not be met by some stern-faced god
who asks of my credit rating
      or
if—I've been good or bad.

No, I believe she will ask me
    the most important questions.

    Did you love?

        Did you care?

        Were you joyful?

            and

    How did you celebrate the splendor
        of this life?

SUTRAS FROM THE INFANT

if

i could
just be
conscious of

the miracle

unfolding

each

moment.

A POEM FOR LISA STEINBERG

Though the newspapers have been folded
and the spring grass covers your grave,
there is an anger
    that refuses to die.

All of this feels like
    a lie
and months later
    tears still come.

Does it do any good to say
    'I'm sorry.'?

Will the millions of words
explain the why or change
    your lonely life?

In some vain gesture I want to
to hold and love you—for one instant.
Yet it is too late...

and still the image of your face
    comes back.

I don't understand...
    I never have.

A part of me wants to hear
that there was some small
piece of joy or simple happiness
    in your very tender life.

If for one instant I could
have held
        or
    loved you.

Yet it seems like more lies—

How many other Lisas are there?
How many now are we not hearing?

Will we again wring our hands,
wipe away the tears,
        and turn the page?

one hundred or more miles from the memory of a wave
which threatened to drown:

we were lying alone.

grey sky, blue, and other pieces.
waves, rise up from within

voracious — thirsty...

devour the sands
and
  the
memories
  of a boy who lived
by the shore

EROS RISING

when I want to devour you

to make love with you
to drink deeply
        the enormous sensuousness
    of love...

is it you
   that I'm loving —

or
  is it

    I?

DAYS

1.

We
frail
objects
cast
to
the
sands.

Tides swell
to
descend,
smoothed
and brutalized...
waves
forge
to the rocks.

Seagulls
with
dinner
in jaw

pull
forth
from
gravity's
(obscene)
lure,
and
crush
plump
stones
in
straight
line
fall...

Split!

Open
awaiting
to be leisurely
eaten.

2.

Feast
exclaimed!

3.

Sun
dries
remnants
and
washes
clean the palate.

White bones
mingle
to
    the sands.

A wave
slithers
    along
and
    retreats.

PEASANT

Hungry

I

till the soil

of these

dreams.

SURRENDER

angels crash
through ceilings

autumn moonlight
　　hangs
its head

we lie

alone

in each other's
　　arms.

IF AN ANGEL:
WOULD SHE SPEAK LIKE YOU?

If we were less of knowing
        and more child-like
in our wonder...
would I be inside you now?

If voices could truly speak
        I would drown your
doubts to slumber and
        shatter the walls
which lie between
    you and I.

Are we too practiced in knowing?
Too well crafted in age?

Or
  is desire merely,
      reticent?

A PILLOW BESIDE ME

i've awakened with lover and partner,
and for sure there is no greater delight.

but there is also a sublime bliss,
    in waking alone...
thoughts—spirit—undistracted.
directly, I move to meditation and typewriter.

directly I move, untethered by the demands
        of this daily human heart.

WELL TURNED PAGE

We see our lives as littered with these roadmarks—
lovers—wives—husbands—children—exs—then—the when which almost
became—the infinitesimal periods of waiting— the buses we missed—the
hours—moments in between—the slow burning—ocean—clear expanse—
land mark ruins wondering how in the hell did we get here—when can we
escape— where is the door—why does the clock keep ticking, like some
sick overused metaphor—age—our bodies falling apart—how we hate the
young—jealous at their sleek moment in the sun (only gleeful in knowing
their turn will come)— when the bills arrive—the checks don't—the
promises are empty sheets of paper—the IOU's are whenever I damn well get
around to paying you—when the children don't write or call—and then
curse yourself for being sentimental—seeing half a life melt into a slow
roll into three/fifths and the fractions which seem to grow ever finer—
the surface beneath, somehow uncertain—you confront—the lies of a life
and haven't a clue how to make sense of any of it— it defies logic—and
certainly expectation ... it is a slide into some abyss that you know for
sure you've visited before. It's a life. Black. White. And for damn sure,
crammed with a freighter load of questions and colours in between.

It is a well-turned page.

NO MIND

the mind is
a very hungry

fox

devouring its own

tail.

very hungry.

THE LOVE SONG OF MR. ROBINSON SMITH

I.

"Mr. Robinson Smith.

Mr. Robinson Smith."

There was no answer.
He heard—but was occupied.
The *Mind Thought Space* which called him was already spoken for.

She lived on an island in the Aegean, almost two hundred and fifty
    years before he was born, with her father and mother who fished the
        seas.
They would rise early in the morning, just before dawn.
The nets would be gathered and the boat's sails raised.

Perhaps in that silence—where there was no time—
    She heard the *Mind Thought Song* of one Mr. Robinson Smith.
    It was his final song.

The poem of an old man who was about to die.

II.

"Mr. Robinson Smith."
"Mr. Robinson Smith."

III.

I have seen summer and now live in the woods
    where leaves deepen to slumbered dreams.

I have seen this life
    and
tasted its colours.

Child, I have held you
like an angel, loved you like a woman,
    and now rock you to sleep with these two arms.

Child
    child
        where might you be?
This life is one part fire
    And wholly memory.

I have lived in these glass towers
And searched through the forest.

This body wears memory
  moment by moment.

Child of the Aegean
I sing my love song to you.

IV.

There was a voice she heard when she walked by the rocks,
    where the sea pours through the narrow channels...

The song reached out

 like a net cast to an infinite sea of years.
When one voice hears it,
    another can die.

Another person will hold the memory of
    who he or she was.

V.

Mind-thought time spans wings across
the centuries. One beat of the wind!
    one pulse of the heart!
     compelled them to soar!
higher —till they dove into a sea
    infinite in dreams.
The child's eyes lifted wide and saw
the sails raised. Full wind filling them.

VI.

There was a lover he once knew
now she was old too.

He saw the face of his children scattered across the galaxy—
     they could not hear him.

This was the time of steel and numbers,
when starships would leap to the far edges
          of the Universe.

He was separating from the known and counted world of molecules and
machines.

He stepped back to the time of poems and dreams.
     and walked though the wall where death
     invites memory
and sleep invites...union.

I dream the dream of infant birth

VII.

Alexandra braids the ropes and recalls the face of an old man
     she met in her dreams.

VIII.

Years later she would write a poem called, *The Love Song of Robinson Smith*.

She told of a dream, which was water deep blue,
when she met the dreamed and imagined thoughts of an old man who
was about to die.

He sang her his song.

The love song each soul leaves to another.

It leaped from the heart of his soul
to the sun center of
     her being.

It was no longer one old man
and a young woman.

In one instant leap across two-hundred and fifty years,
two souls met— like pools of sun-light converging—
     and made love.

> "Mr. Robinson Smith...
> Mr. Robinson Smith."

But there was no reply.

He was gone,

     his song had been spoken.

burning into revelation

1.

   if
I saw each breath

   word

and
   ripple of thought
as
   the still connection
of
   I to I
in
   continual revelation—

2.

deep lavender lies
   succulent
next to a flame red leaf.

a breeze surfs, without
   inhibition
across my face.

3.

if.

4.

burning
   into
revelation.

SEED

1.

did you ever
...wonder

  of
  a
seed's power?

an instigation of genius,
spark of some casual insight
  or
god-head lurking?

2.

... the acorn
which explodes
towards heaven,

  the crocus
which invites Spring
  or
the sublime brilliance
  of an infant's
enormous thirsty eyes?

3.

did you ever
... wonder
  of
  a
seed's power?

THE FACE OF A MAN TRYING TO UNDERSTAND

I do not often understand this feeling of being a man

there are too many lies,
too many false beginnings
  of what this thing is to be a man.

When I look into the Adonis face
  of my son
I see my questions of what it is
  to be a man...
At sixteen in the first steps of asking
his own questions.

I speak to my father,
and wonder when he will say,
    I love you.
Is his the generation numbed by duty,
muted by the weight of manhood?

I am a man who sees the woman
inside,
and celebrates her presence.

I am a man who rejoices when
he can meet and love
another on equal terms...
no walls ... only the bridge of
        simple
human understanding.

Why do we so often deny the immense
    capability of love?

I am a man who embraces being a man...
with all the doubt, ambiguity, and longing
this human soul
  can hold.

I am a man coming forth
into my full, beautiful,
  humanness;

Be patient,
  I will be there soon.

NEARER

a stone falls
   into
the pond—

smooth
concentric
circles

which
elegantly
touches
the
shore.

when
will
i reach—

You?

I WAKE UP ALONE

yesterday's lover
   some
miles away.

odd,
   how quickly
fire burns.

THROUGH THESE EYES WHICH HOLD YOU AND ME

When you wore
   my glasses
did you see
   through my eyes?

Did you see heaven,
   the way that I wear it
And the moon,
      when she lies
     blissful on the Overlook?
Or starlight,
   which speaks
     incantations to this soul?

If I wore
   your garments of silk and rough wool...
would I hold
   the wind in my teeth,
     like you?
Would I laugh
     when alone
and cry when
    you were there?

What would I wear
    when I wear you?

What would we see
    when we wore each other?

HARVEST

Pumpkin season sky
  unfurls like a clean fresh sheet;
Palest of blue-
  Single songed note of a flute.

Attention is riveted,
    by the leaf burnt, apple ripe,
tart sensation of the wind.

What whispered voice memory
    of fire
compels the virulent...succulent
  green to surrender?

What wind spun incantation invites
  the Fall,
and shouts down the
  fortressed and sheltering green?

Why has the roots' driven thirst
    for the sun
    surrendered
to the shivering naked limbs?

Why does the pumpkin season sky
    bleed
into the sullen leafed earth,

And how has the moon spoken
  to your ancient soul?

INFANT STEPS

What is a child, but an awakening of a dream,
a revelation of ourselves.

Who is the child that lives inside?
What are the fears and unspoken tears?

Will the cry of our aloneness
        awaken the child?
Or, will she cause us to fear,
    even more,
our unseen needs?

Child inside show me these slumbering
        worlds of fear and pain, I've yet to own!

For,
    if I could live within a space in this life,
        it would not be as a doer or maker,
                but as a joyful creator;

a child, constantly awakening
to the splendor of the Universe.

MY WORKSHOP

Linseeding
   birch panels —
long
   loving strokes.

Brother Marley
   sings
clear and sweet.

I dance
   &
linseed
   some more.

The rain
   falls
   step by
step.

I dance and
   work.

homeless

nothing more basic

than the desire...

no!

not desire,

but the deep bone-rooted need,

to have a place

of one's own.

DREAMS OF THE NUDE GODDESS

Spring green fire
    enraptures
this sullen flushed — passion.

Beneath shadow—
    lies
       these driven desires:

   Naked.

I have swung on the trees
    and launched myself skyward—
but was enraged
     to be lured, to earth
    once again.

I am seduced
     by the sinewed and lush,
    erotic green!

And i have seen the face
    of god as she lies

    serene,

on cool spring hills.

DELICIOUS

Sunlight washes over me,
cool breeze intermingles.

I stop and listen
   to the two —

to my heart —
   and this soul,
     breathing.

How delicious
   to be alive!
To be alive in this instant
   without thought —

Just being!

How indescribably delicious.

NO DOUBT IN MY MIND

No doubt in my mind when she came into the room.
Instinctively I smoothed my hair and checked my cool.
At least the former was in place,
But for the rest of me—I admit—it was instant over-boil.

No doubt in my mind: It was Love at first sight
and amorous adventures in a silken wonderland.

My mind reeled through every successful script I could conjure,
    'The forlorn poet?'
'Hell no, she would never fall for that.'
    'The smooth and urbane wit?'
I'm short on both these days
Though perhaps the empathic soul—the sensitive caring hand...

Or just to blurt it out, "I'm sorry, though we've just met, and know
this is a bit crass: Will you marry me? Let us make our honeymoon nest
on the spot without delay, and tomorrow we'll marry."

"Oh, you're married? Three children?
Maybe we can make a compromise. Forget the wedding and we'll just
        settle for the honeymoon."

"Children will be home from school soon?"

Gee... it's funny,
    There was no doubt in my mind, when we first met.

SUNDOWN

I am a sucker for sunsets

and love to watch them
  long after they've gone.

It's not just the burning brilliance,
  but the power of the dying

which holds such fascination;

even when the chill has set in
  and the sun's warmth has long faded.

We bleed into each other's pain
  and watch the night devour the light.

SIRI

baby buddha
master
age
20 months

starlight
spun
from
human
love.

THE TASTE OF WINTER

Her thighs are very warm, but her ass is
    so cold.
Hold me close. Winter is coming soon.

The gaps in the mud filled walls,
    whistle ice tipped blue.
The chill becomes a ghost in search
    of the fireplace;

I too.

The apple wood burns in the stove, and I
remember the bitter taste of a seed in
    my mouth.
How sweet is a flower?
How delicious her perfume?

When will I hold her again?

I am hungry and feast on sourdough bread, honey,
    and fresh made yogurt.
I am thirsty and drink her down like a jug
    of cold wine.

I devour you in slow bites and
    savor each untasted morsel.

LOVE POEM TO KRISHNAMURTI

I have burned all your books
   but not forgotten what you said.

Instead of opening to a page—
I now turn to the enchanted
   blaze of the fall.

Your voice trickles mellifluously
   in the most intimate space of my soul.
I cannot nor do I want—to erase it.

It whispers, *Look!*

       Listen!

     Be Awed!

Should I have remembered more?

   I think not.

SIMPLE BOUQUET

I will make
    you a bouquet, not of roses,
but wildflowers and seagrasses
    that grow
      close
to the abandoned cottage.

Beneath this stark and slender
    silvered
       moon

I will undress your
      sleeping desires,

    unhurried,

like a wave
    at
      low tide
that lazily rolls
across the wet
    supple sand.

And if we are angels meant
    to fly,
      so be it...

I am too old for illusion,
      but fertile for
dreaming.

I will make you
    this bed —

not of reveries
    nor imaginings

but these
    simple desires —

      come.

WONDER

I wonder
how wide the deep blue erotic sky,
And how a god crafted
the sensuous wave of a tree?

And how delicious
it must be to be that breeze,

that slides along her
 lean
  slender
     thighs.

I wonder.

SUMMER BORN TOO SOON

Winter quickens.
Shuttered in clothes too dull to own.
She comes sullen faced and
     teary eyed;
a child bruised from ventures
     near the breaker.

Forecasts of snow hang ripe on
     the vine.
Farmers say, "This year ... soon."
Poets, forever out of time, will not own
     the moment;

     Passing!

The news of a death is not cause
     for celebration!

     Passing!

Squirrels, sail across
     tree tops:
Grey arms padding
     the sky's belly:
Sultry supple limbs kneed the
     thirst to be loved.

Nude! Waiting for shrouds.

Hooded and in mourning clothes:
     Should we chant kaddish?
       Vigil?
Or, own revelation and discover
     our first infant voice at birth:

Now, muffled by the throbbing pulse of memory..

Are we made: holy,
  divine,
or just plain slush grey mad—
by the yet
        white fallen snow?

Pulse.   Muscle.   Blood.
Roots driven. Supple green. Rushing towards heaven

Memory!

We carry you. Memory ! We breathe you.
Memory! We have given you. Memory!

In the still-born hours
we wear shrouds and curse the unknown.

We damn the past and allow it to drown
 our known & waking desires.

Borne to summer!

Born among the shards
    of broken light!

Waves stretch : languid: sullen : greased
    from starving steel barges.

In a trip of a moment, turn of the page,
    and the unexpected parting of the curtain:

Sun surprised! Leaped! Devoured! Swept clean the
night.

A child laughs, naked, running
    across hot white sands.

Her footsteps form our dance upon the shore-line.
Summer memory shapes the prayer.
The anger ache of isolation,
    is the Spirit of our chants.

    God-head made human.

    Glorious!

      Nude!

    Dancing!

LET THE ELVES DANCE!

Kindergarten children, elves wrapped in
    blue, pink, and rainbow pastels;
holding hands, and being just children.

The school marm roars, "Don't touch anything!
Line up. If you break anything we'll take
your name and tell your parents!"

Fear! Do we teach fear or do we teach love?
Do we have the courage —
the audacity —
the boldness of spirit
  to teach love?

If this is socialization,
  then, give me naked
freedom.

Why do we teach by fear?

Give the children a garden!

A forest to play in!
And miles of space to roam and dream,
    untethered by fear...

And able to wander in the infinite
    joyous space of love.

Let the elves dance and be free!

DIVORCE

we were exhausted, too long struggling to
remember

when we loved.

when love was the sun center of our universe
and we —
    were fearless.

what do we now say
when others ask — 'Why?'

was it a loss of faith?
the children?   money?

or was it a failure of memory?

when passion was at each breath

and we hungered for more.

SHORELINE

I slept in the womb warm sands and dreamed
   of her, who wept and walked on these shores.

I dreamed the splendor of her spirit,
and breathed the vastness of an
   ocean and the single
     joy of holding her close.

Winter weaved between
this rapture and longing;
   I who held on to knowing,
      surrendered to loving.

Tides return
   and evening hurries near.
We huddle close and build a fire
   from the remnant pieces
      gathered along the shore.

Darkness quickens.

We end the need to speak
   and
curl together,
   two question marks lying on the shore.

We impressed
   on the sand these desires;
now swept smooth of memory and longing.

RED CAPES   WHITE FLAGS

Why do I so often
  surrender
     to
anger and violence:

instead of the
  innocent
    knowing
      of love?

How do I surrender
  this ego

to a greater
  unfolding.

CIRCLE OF COLOURS

I.

What are the colours to these emotions?

Though I know red, yellow,
    and green, somehow the jaundiced
netherworld
    and the ruby beacons of Neustrasse
    are more patient,
      more alluring than being
  alone.

Red lipped. Pouting. Thirsty.
Each window passed, a portal for
    this soul's lurid imagination.
And when the curtains were drawn, pink
    wombed lights flooded the room.

I was drowning.
In this dense collage, where
    feelings and sensations
      collide, and then disintegrate

Love? I saw her along the side-street, beneath the
    street lamp. Demure. Conservative. Looking
      as if she was waiting for one of the lost
  boys; instead of leading them to a new turn.

She would lead them upstairs. Their faces flushed, eyes darting,
    attentive and vulnerable, too young to anticipate
a trap, or an exchange.

      Innocence for a new garment?

It happens all the time. One says love and the other
    is counting the change.

She lives apart from the others; yet, each evening she
    is there.

One night I followed.

At middle-age what was I trying to discover?

The lights were lowered, I undressed, and so did she,
    partially.

I was hungry and tired, she held me in her smooth strong arms.
    Only later did I realize why he didn't charge me.

The ruse.

Love wears many colours.

II.

There is a place where the river
    pours out of the city.
An old canal house, now used by Zen monks,
    who chant their prayers in Dutch and English.

I made a circle of beads, each bead was crafted from an image
    found. One of the broken lights on Neustrasse, a condom,
    a piece of broken red-high heel, a penny whistle, a scrap of
    paper with a phone number—blurred by the rain, and so
    on until the chain stretched as wide as a man's belt.

Counting beads I would sing prayers, poems, doggerels, and
    children's rhymes as I walked along the city streets...
past Oued Kirk and carnivals.

I called each bead a colour — in Dutch, Spanish, English, or in
    whatever language came to mind. Each one became an age.
    Each age became a memory.
        Until I could no longer stand the pain. Black and blue at ten.
Red faced at eight. Cold blue and shivering at four. Then I

    receded further.

Today, I made a necklace, it was the sound of unremembered emotions.

When I whirled it round above my head, it arced, like a spun
    circle of gold.
When I wore it around my neck, it revealed the colours in people's
    eyes. So often I saw the stark black and blue, the bruises well creased
        into each soul.

Most often it was easier to keep it in my hands. Like prayer
    beads. But more supple. Tender.

For each year of this life, I've counted a sensation—a colour I
    didn't know existed.

The woman or man, who stood beneath the street-lamp, showed me
    one which was more than terrifying,

it was the colour when we are naked and alone for the very first time.

One day by the shore, when sunlight was trying to arrive, I turned
    and heard something in the wind. I thought it was a young girl
    laughing.

I started to cry when I realized it was the very first
    sound I ever made .
Neither laughter, nor tears, but
  a shout of stark amazement
    like in ... whoa! How did I get here?

III.

It is snowing now. The red-brick buildings whiten, and the sky
    betrays no clue.

IV.

I count these beads,

    one by one.

BLACKBIRD

I have impaled myself on anger.
Twisted and torn myself apart,
Like a crow caught on a rusted barbed wire.

Stupid bird!
Who could fly so high
Yet, chose to eviscerate
itself on the wire.

AN ANGEL WHO FEEDS ON HUNGER

is like
a
cloud that feeds
on
love.

It
is
raining.

EMPTY HOUSE ON THE BEACH

september.

   wide, open
    faces
     laughing

dark skin
   blond hair
wool shawl
   drawn tight;
sunset—
   orange
    violet colours.

long wave, runs
   upon the beach
then slips away.
a breaker cracks.

we sleep on
   the sands;

pink—
   deep, blue
    skies.

PROMETHEUS

Poets
fly off
buildings
and
drown

to

awaken

again
&
again.

an emptiness in this life

awoke to find the
        morning sun,
stretched across
    my empty bed.

saw this life as a
    set of memories —

lovers — wives and
    the long intervals between.

birds in the trees,
    and the green new born leaves —
shout temptation —

    to the bright blue sky.

ZEN — ZEN — WHITE BONES

Zen flower
red lipped — green stemmed
fragranced.

No Zen.
No Flower.
Only,

    white bones.

        twenty minutes

if this life had to end in twenty
minutes —

would it be spent writing a poem?
making love?
or sitting in meditation?

waterline

it is afterall
how we love or hate —
that the difference is made.

it is dignity and faith
        that holds the spirit
together

it is loving and then —
letting go

to surrender
    and
embrace.

a paradox,
    surely.

life.

MOSES AND THE FORTY YEAR DETOUR

I understand the metaphor so well.
Life outside the promised land is
   the wilderness,
and the promised land is
   our on-going
daily meditation and discovery.

It is when I'm meditating
   and conscious that my
life is a spiritual journey,
   then there is a real peace
      and serenity.

Otherwise, it is chaos without
   sense or reason...
Just a succession of events
   bound together —
called a life.

How mundane!
   How profound the difference.

notes of the hunter

as men we are trained
  to do one of
two things —
to conquer

 or
kill it.

please,
understand
the enormous
and
painful difficulty
of being
  a
man.

WHEN IS IT TIME TO BITE THE HAND THAT FEEDS YOU

gurus enchant the senses
and we are delighted as hell,
to know truth is so near.
in as far as knowing can
        be tasted —
and savored like
    fresh roasted meat.

when the *Master* tells us —
do we leap like hungry dogs
    to the dinner plate?
are we so easily sated?

is it easier to lick
        the hand of one who opens the can,

        or

do I choose to run for the
    open meadow
        gate?

SUM OF THE EQUATION

I am not made like
  a shadow against the wall.

But created as an image
   spun from light
     and

Ascended into
  being.

Not angel. Not satyr.

But more mystical—

  Human.

SECULAR PRAYERS

not in blind recitation to some

created deity,

but simply
to Be
Awake
and conscious of the miracle,

unfolding each

moment.

RYAN'S DHARMA DEMONSTRATION
OF EATING A PEANUT BUTTER SANDWICH

Three years old,
    the Master, teaches me
how to really eat
    a peanut-butter sandwich.

Two tiny hands,
    clutch
a slice of bread-
    and peanut—butter.

Discovery!

The dharma of attention—instant
    focus!
Long tongue leap
    down the center, giggle!
And laughter at the sensation
    running
on his tongue.

RED UNION SUIT ON A SNOWY WINTER DECEMBER DAY

if i were a healer, open to loving,
   would I hear you cry?
would I sense your needs
   before mine?

if i saw my anger less
as righteousness and god's will
   made writ—
would i then begin to heal?

if i were open to hearing
not only my words, but the
violence and aloneness they caused ...
would i then be silent?

this anger, my ego,
a red union suit stretched on a clothes line
on a snowy december day.

if i surrendered this vain desire and
heard instead
this child's need for love and attention—
would i turn my arms inward and
   rock this child to
     wholeness?

NU

... dare to speak
with dreams,
expose our cherished

   icons ...

 empty
the known —
   and
stand nude?

Can we ridicule
who we are? What we believe?

Not from nobility
or vain narcissism —
but
                hunger.

Do we
                    dare
to wander without direction
   or
   home —

attentive
            vulnerable

and

in

   splendor?

QUAKER SUNDAY MORNING

meeting house, freshly hewn,
    simple New England lines.

the hearth simmers warm.

spirit lean, abundant, and
    sun-lit
december morning, a clear sense of meeting,
    here in the snow.

sky whitens!

when the Spirit speaks there is
    a soul stirring righteousness.

but when the spirit heals
it is felt in the sensuous silent
    fall of snow.

Quaker Sunday morning.

PEACE SHRINES

I dreamed of a day,
while I was awake.

Missile silos, each one of them
became a peace shrine.
Like the small shrines that dot
rural Europe.

How many are there?

Each surrounding village,
community, today, or soon tomorrow
would celebrate the
renaissance.

Once deep holes of fear,
now abiding wells of hope.

moving into wholeness

i am not alone

i am here

with my self

at peace —

listening

still

&

attentive.

SOON

I believe that when the poet and
    philosopher speak a common language

then the New Era will begin.

When the scientist can understand what the mystic says

and the physician touches with the hands of a healer

when the carpenter reverences a tree
    as much as a woodsman
when a minister can hear the song of spirit

when the need for hunger and desire for war has fled

when the earth and sky are remembered as sacred

    And we recall

    the first spoken

      blessing
      of
Gaia — Great Mother Spirit —

then, the New Age will have begun.

I CELEBRATE THE BODY-SPIRIT!

1.

I celebrate the Body-Spirit
and exclaim the child-like awe
        of my soul leaping to discover
not new green vistas, nor uncharted wildernesses.
But the primal ecstasy of my being
        enveloped in the sheer
                sensuous
                bliss

        of awakening-

        BODY!

        SPIRIT!

            this

            SOUL

        AWAKENING!

2.

EARTH—

    I have slept in the womb-stirred revery of the wind

    Which compels green leaves

        to remember!

    (And too ____ me.)

WIND !

    The ripe August breeze lifts
        high the hem of her dress
    And rushes finger-like waves
        through her auburn hair.

FIRE !

When our bodies touch.

WATER.

We can not quench desire
    with water,
Nor feed spirit with
    food.

Green seaweed tide slithers along the edge,
    and then fades back into the
    faceless sea.

3.

I was lying bare assed — beautiful naked
    on an immense green lawn
blissed out on the sweet tender blue of the sky

infant like enthralled
        by the erotic sway
of full leafed maple trees.

Lovers passed by and giggled.

A little boy saw me, and
  he and his sister threw off
their clothes. I was delighted!

A cop clad in deep blue (in spirit and cloth), red-faced —
        DEMANDED to know what I was doing.

What am I doing?

"I am celebrating this day."

"But you're naked!"

I could not argue with such a keen intellect and simply said,

        "YES, I AM NAKED!"

I plucked a dandelion and made a wish that his
    blue iron-clad suit would melt
        like
    fresh chocolate in the hot sun.

I then placed the stem across my Venus-blessed arch.

He failed to see the humor, much to my regret,
    and so with a salubratory leap

    I danced across the lawn
in the full splendor of the late August sun.

4.

    I

  SING!

  SHOUT!

  DANCE!

  BREATHE!

this deep rooted erotic
  spirituality!

Not only in the sensuous roar of sunlight

But when the full moon rises
    I stoop down on my haunches
raise my head back
    and from the pit of my soul
howl at the moon.

5.

I have yet to discover
    all the ways
to express this being...

I celebrate
        even in times of anguish and doubt,

And when confronted with the willful making
        of human madness and tragedy

I celebrate this too.

I celebrate
        what we need to become —

        BODY!

            SPIRIT!

        SOUL!

Awakening to the simple
        splendor
            of —

        Being!

ABOUT THE AUTHOR

Thom Namayá—Is a Zen-Quaker poet and performance artist who lives in the Lower Hudson Valley. His poetry and short-stories have appeared in a wide range of magazines from *Radical America* to the Australian publication *Simply Living*. He is also known for his electrifying stand-up poetry performances, which he has presented throughout the United States.

His current project is creating a multi-media poem for the six senses.

In addition to his work as a writer, Thom is a trainer/consultant for nonprofit organizations and offers the workshop "Survival Training for Human Services."